DATE DUE

Classifying Flowering Plants

FRANCINE D. GALKO

Heinemann Library
Chicago, Illinois

Designed by Heinemann Library
Illustrated by Carrie Gowran
Photo research by Kathryn Creech
Printed in China

08 07 06 05
10 9 8 7 6 5 4 3

Library of Congress Cataloging-in-Publication Data
Galko, Francine.
  Flowering plants / by Francine Galko.
    v. cm. -- (Classifying living things)
  Includes bibliographical references and index.
  Contents: The variety of life -- What are
  flowering plants? -- What do flowering plants
  look like? -- Flowering plant classes --
  Magnolias and their relatives -- Oaks and their
  relatives -- Meat-eating plants and their
  relatives -- Roses and their relatives -- Palms
  and their relatives -- Grasses, sedges, and
  their relatives -- Lilies, orchids, and their
  relatives -- Recognizing flowering plants.
   ISBN 1-4034-3272-4 (Hardcover) --
   ISBN 1-4034-3276-7 (Paperback)
  1. Plants--Juvenile literature. 2. Angiosperms-
  -Juvenile literature.[1. Plants. 2. Angiosperms.
  3. Flowers.] I. Title. II. Series.
   QK49.G33 2003
   580--dc21

2003004977

Acknowledgments
The author and publishers are grateful to
the following for permission to reproduce
copyright material:

p. 4 George D. Lepp/Corbis; p. 5 Kenneth R.
Robertson, Ph.D./Illinois Natural History
Survey; p. 6 Tania Midgley/Corbis; pp. 7, 9,
22 Corbis; p. 8 Japack Company/Corbis; p. 10
John M. Roberts/Corbis; p. 12 Hal
Horwitz/Corbis; p. 13 Doug Sokell/Visuals
Unlimited, Inc.; p. 14 Neil Miller/Papilio/
Corbis; p. 15 Science VU/Visuals Unlimited,
Inc.; p. 16 Richard Shiell/Earth Scenes; p. 17
Brian Rogers/Visuals Unlimited, Inc.; p. 18 Ed
Horn/Taxi/Getty Images; p. 19 Robert
Pickett/Corbis; p. 20 Kjell B. Sandved/Visuals
Unlimited, Inc.; p. 21 Mark S. Skalny/Visuals
Unlimited, Inc.; p. 23 Richard Thom/Visuals
Unlimited, Inc.; p. 24 Peter Smithers/Corbis;
p. 25 Paul A. Zahl/National Geographic/Getty
Images; p. 26 Steve Terrill/ Corbis; p. 27
Cooke, J. A. L./OSF/Animals Animals; p. 28
Bill Beatty/Visuals Unlimited, Inc.; p. 29
Michelle Garrett/Corbis

Cover photograph by Eric Crichton/Corbis

Special thanks to Jack Shouba, botany
instructor at the Morton Arboretum, and
Kenneth R. Robertson, Illinois Natural History
Survey, for their help in the preparation of
this book.

Every effort has been made to contact
copyright holders of any material reproduced
in this book. Any omissions will be rectified in
subsequent printings if notice is given to the
publisher.

Some words are shown in bold, **like this.** You can find out what they mean by looking in the glossary.

Contents

The Variety of Life

Earth is populated with a great variety of living things, from the tallest sequoia tree to microscopic **bacteria**. Scientists believe all these organisms—including humans—are the **descendants** of one group of simple organisms that lived millions of years ago. Some of these organisms are flowering plants. Scientists can identify more than 250,000 different **species** of flowering plants, and many more are thought to still be undiscovered. To try to understand how flowering plants might be related to one another and to other plants, scientists **classify** them.

Flowering plants come in many sizes and shapes. You can see tulips and purple hyacinths in this flower garden.

Sorting the living world

When you sort something, you need to do it in a useful way. Scientists try to classify living things in a way that tells how closely one group of plants or animals is related to another. To do this, they compare groups of living things with one another. They look at everything about the living thing, from its color and shape to the **genes** inside its **cells.** Then they use all this information to sort the millions of different living things into groups.

A species is a single kind of plant or animal, such as a loblolly pine tree or a domestic dog. Species that are very similar to one other are put together in a larger group called a **genus,** or genera, if there is more than one. For example, all pine trees are in the genus *Pinus.* Genera that are similar to one another are grouped into **families**, and similar families make up larger groups called **orders.**

Closely related orders are grouped into **classes.** Classes are arranged into groups that are usually called **phyla,** or phylum if there is only one. However, plant biologists use the word **division** instead of phylum. Like phyla, divisions are organized into huge groups called **kingdoms.** All plants, for example, are in one kingdom—the plant kingdom.

Scientific names

Many living things have a common name. Common names are not always exact. They change from place to place. People in different places use names familiar to their region. Names can also change from country to country due to language differences. When scientists classify living things, they give every species a two-part scientific name. Scientific names are in Latin and are recognized by scientists all over the world. The first part of the scientific name tells you the genus that the living thing belongs to. The second part of the name tells you the species within the genus.

Plantae (Plants) — Kingdom

Magnoliophyta (Angiosperms) — Division

Magnoliopsida (Dicots) — Class

Rosales (Roses and their relatives) — Order

Rosaceae (Rose family) — Family

Rosa (Roses) — Genus

Rosa carolina (Carolina Rose) — Species

This diagram shows the classification for a Rosa carolina, such as the one pictured here.

What Are Flowering Plants?

Flowering plants make up their own **division** in the plant **kingdom.** Flowering plants make **seeds** as well as flowers and **fruits.** There are two main kinds of seed plants within the flowering plant kingdom: **gymnosperms** and **angiosperms.**

Gymnosperms make "naked seeds," such as the seeds in a pine cone. Unlike fruits, pine cones open up and expose their seeds to the air when they are mature and the weather is good for growth. Gymnosperms are thought to be the **ancestors** of flowering plants.

Flowering plants are called angiosperms. Unlike gymnosperms, angiosperms enclose their seeds in fruits. Angiosperms are a very successful group of plants. In fact, they make up most of the plant kingdom. Of the approximately 300,000 living plant **species,** more than 250,000 belong to the angiosperm division. Most of the plants around you are angiosperms. Angiosperms grow almost everywhere on land—even in difficult growing conditions on the islands off the continent of Antarctica—and in many water environments. Orchids and bromeliads are usually found in tropical regions. Angiosperms live in more **habitats** than any other group of plants.

Gladiolus are commonly planted in flower gardens. You might have seen these flowers at the supermarket or at a flower stand. Gladiolus make complete flowers. Their flowers have all four whorls—sepals, petals, stamens, and pistils. Can you find all four whorls on the gladiolus in this photo?

Like many watermelons, this one has large black seeds inside. Some people coat the seeds with spices and eat them. Others use the seeds for spitting contests. But most people just eat around the seeds. That's why plant scientists have developed new kinds of watermelons that have either small seeds, or none at all.

Four Whorls

A flower can be divided into four circles. Each circle is called a **whorl.** Petals make up one whorl. Under the petals of some flowers are tiny green structures that look like leaves. They are called **sepals.** Sepals make up the outermost whorl. Male **reproductive** parts, called **stamens,** make up the third whorl. Female reproductive parts, called **pistils,** make up the fourth whorl. The reproductive parts are inside the petals.

A flower that has all four whorls—sepals, petals, stamens, and pistils—is called a **complete flower.** Not all flowers have all four sets of parts. If any whorl is missing, the flower is called an **incomplete flower.** Some flowers, such as tulips, have both male and female reproductive parts. These flowers are called **perfect flowers.** A perfect flower could still be missing sepals or petals and be incomplete.

Other flowers have either male or female parts. Flowers with only one kind of reproductive part are called **imperfect flowers.** Imperfect flowers are also incomplete flowers since they are missing one of the four whorls.

Pollinating Flowers

You may have noticed that some flowers have bright colors or give off a strong scent. Colors, odors, and **nectar** are some ways that flowers attract insects or other animals. When an insect drinks a flower's nectar, the insect may become coated with **pollen.** The insect can then carry the pollen to another flower. This process is called **pollination.**

Fruits

A **fruit** is a ripened female **reproductive** part of a flower. Fruits protect **seeds** and often help them travel to new places. Some flowering plants, such as dandelions and maple trees, have seeds in fruits that are shaped like kites or propellers. Wind can easily carry these seeds to new places. Other flowering plants have seeds in fruits shaped like **burrs.** These seeds attach to animal fur or human clothing. When an animal eats a fruit, seeds pass through the **digestive system** of the animal and are deposited in a new place to grow.

The seeds of dandelions are in fruits shaped like tiny parachutes. The wind carries these seeds away. When the seed reaches a new place suitable for growing, it grows into a new dandelion plant.

What Do Flowering Plants Look Like?

The body of a flowering plant has three main parts: roots, stems, and leaves. Each part has a specific function to help the plant survive.

Roots

Roots are usually the part of a plant that grows under the ground. Roots hold a plant in place. Roots also take in water and **minerals** from the soil around them. The roots then pass the water and minerals on to the plant's stem. The roots of some plants store food for the plant.

Roots grow only from their ends. The tip of a root is covered with a little protective cap. The root cap protects the root as it grows through dirt.

Stems

Stems do not always look alike, but you can usually recognize them because they are growing up from the ground. **Angiosperm** stems usually have flowers and leaves or branches growing out from them. The trunk of a tree is a stem. The main stalk of a plant connecting the plant's roots and its leaves is also a stem.

The hibiscus flower is the state flower of Hawaii. Although people as far north as Canada grow these flowers in their gardens, hibiscus grow best in warm, moist tropical areas. Red, pink, and yellow flowers are common. Hibiscus flowers also come in lavender, blue, white, brown, gold, and a dark red that looks black.

Cactuses are native to North and South America and are adapted to dry areas. Their thick stems are usually green and carry out photosynthesis. They may have no leaves, or just small spines instead of green leaves. Their thin roots grow close to the surface of the ground, where they take in water from dew and occasional rains. Most scientists think that the cactuses growing in other parts of the world were brought there from North and South America.

Stems move water and **nutrients** from one part of a plant to its other parts. Some green stems also make food by the process of **photosynthesis.** Other stems store food. For example, potatoes are underground stems, called **tubers.** Some stems, such as those on rose bushes, have thorns on them. Thorns help protect a plant from animals. The stems of cactuses are usually thick and can store water.

Leaves

Leaves are usually flat and green. They grow out from stems. Leaves carry out photosynthesis and make food for the entire plant. Not all leaves look alike. Some leaf **adaptations** allow plants to climb, store water or nutrients, fend off **predators,** trap and **digest prey,** or adjust to **climate.** For example, the leaves on a cactus are long spikes. These spikes prevent animals from eating the plant. They also collect water in the form of dew. The dew forms on the spikes and drips to the ground. Then it soaks into the ground and the cactus's roots take it in. Other plant leaves, such as those on aloe and hen-and-chick plants, are thick and store water.

Flowering Plant Classes

There are about 250,000 living **species** of **angiosperms**. They are grouped into two main **classes: monocots** and **dicots**.

Two classes of flowering plants

Flowering plants are divided into two classes based on how many seed leaves, or **cotyledons**, they have. Seed leaves are the leaves a plant grows when it is still an **embryo** inside a **seed**. Flowering plants with two seed leaves are called dicotyledons, or dicots. Those with only one seed leaf are called monocotyledons, or monocots.

The orders

Monocot and dicot classes are divided into **orders**. There are many orders of flowering plants. Dicots are usually divided into more than 50 orders. Monocots are divided into more than 15 orders. Only some of these orders are discussed here. To learn more, you might talk to a gardener or join a gardening club. You can also learn a lot about flowering plants at a nearby botanical garden or arboretum.

	Monocots	Dicots
Seed leaves	one seed leaf corn seed	two seed leaves bean seed
Flowers	flower parts in multiples of four or five day lily	flower parts in multiples of three evening primrose
Leaf veins	leaf veins are parallel grass leaf	leaf veins form a net pattern maple leaf
Roots	fibrous roots grass root	taproot dandelion root
Examples	corn, day lily, iris, wheat, camas	bean, rose, sunflower, violet, maple, water lily

Magnolias and Their Relatives

Magnolias, paw paw, and nutmeg are related to the earliest-known flowering plants. These plants tend to be either woody bushes, climbing plants, or trees. They are grouped together in the magnolia **order** mainly because they have some ancient features that plants in other orders no longer have.

All members of this group are **dicots**—they have two seed leaves. Members of this group are found all over the world. They live in both wet and dry areas. Some have leaves that are coated with wax. The wax helps keep water inside the plant.

The world's oldest flowering plant

The oldest known flowering plant lived 140 million years ago. A **fossil** of this **extinct** plant was found in China. Some scientists think that this plant grew in shallow water at the same time that dinosaurs lived on Earth.

The first-known flowering plants are related to today's magnolia trees. If you live in the southeastern part of the United States, then you might have seen or smelled a magnolia tree. These trees make very strong, sweet-smelling flowers. But the oldest flowering plants did not look like magnolia trees at all. Their flowers did not even have petals. Their **seeds** were enclosed in flowering structures that may have developed like magnolias.

Magnolia fruits are shaped like cones. Their seeds are often red and hang by threads.

Oaks and Their Relatives

Oak trees belong to the oak order within the dicots. The leaves on these trees have net-like **veins,** which is a characteristic of dicots. Most of the members of this group are common flowering trees. Examples include oak, beech, chestnut, birch, hazelnut, and hornbeam. The flowers on these trees tend to be very small and green. They do not have **nectar** or fragrance.

Falling leaves

You have probably noticed that some trees, such as oaks, lose their leaves in the fall. These trees are called **deciduous** trees. Deciduous trees stop growing in winter. This helps them to avoid drying out since roots cannot get water from frozen ground. By dropping leaves, the trees avoid water loss through their leaves and keep more water inside the plant.

Related forms

Some orders related to oaks include walnut, hickory, elm, mulberry, and barberry. These plants are **classified** together because they tend to have separate male and female flowers. Their **pollen** is usually carried by the wind.

Tree garlands

Oaks and most of their relatives are **pollinated** by wind. Wind carries the pollen from male flowers to female flowers. These flowers usually do not have an odor. Often the flowers are small. You might not even recognize them as flowers. Many small male flowers form long, powdery chains that dangle from the trees. The female flowers are larger and open, allowing them to catch the pollen in the wind.

Oak trees in the United States pollinate from February until June. During pollination, wind carries pollen for miles to flowers linked in a chain called a catkin. Some people are allergic to oak pollen. Oak pollen can cause sneezing, runny nose, and itchy, watery eyes.

Insect-eating plants

You probably know that some insects eat plants. But did you know that some plants eat insects? There are about 200 **species** of meat-eating plants in the **dicots.** They include the Venus's flytrap, the pitcher plant, and the sundew. They live in areas where the soil is poor. These plants use their leaves to trap insects. Trapping insects and absorbing **nutrients** from the insect bodies allows the plants to get nutrients that are not present in the soil.

Insect-eating plants have different ways of catching insects. Pitcher plants form a deep cup with their leaves. The hoodlike leaf that covers the deep cup gives off a strong smell that attracts insects. When the insects come to the leaf, they fall into the pitcher, where they are **digested.**

*The leaves of a Venus's flytrap form a snapping trap. Tiny hairs on the surface of the leaves signal the leaves to close around **prey** inside the trap. Digestive juices break down the insect's body and the plant absorbs the nutrients.*

Stringy fungi living on and in a plant's roots help the plant get minerals from the soil. Like waiters at a restaurant, the fungi bring minerals in the soil right to the plant's roots. Many fungi also act as extra roots on a plant. The more roots a plant has, the more minerals it can soak up and move to other parts of the plant.

The leaves of sundew plants are covered with sticky red hairs. When an insect lands on the hairs, it gets stuck. Then, the leaf curls around the insect and digests it.

The leaves of a Venus's flytrap are hinged like a trap door. When the tiny hairs on the surface of the leaves are touched, the leaves snap shut. This traps any insect that might have touched the leaves inside. The insect's body is digested inside the trap.

Fungi-friendly plants

Fungi live on the roots of some plants in this group. They include azaleas, rhododendrons, blueberries, and cranberries. Some of these plants cannot survive without fungi. Others can live without fungi, but they are healthier when the fungi live on and in their roots. Long threads of fungi grow all around and even inside the plant roots. The fungi and plant roots often look like a big tangle of string.

By living on or in the roots, the fungi and the roots are able to exchange food and **minerals.** The fungi get food from the plants' roots. Food that the plant makes by **photosynthesis** moves from the roots into the fungi. Fungi provides minerals from the soil directly to the plants. These minerals move from the fungi into the plant's roots.

Roses and Their Relatives

Another group of **dicots** is the rose **order** and its related orders. Many plants related to roses are well known for their beauty or **fruit.** You might be surprised that many plants in this group do not look like roses.

The leaves on these plants usually have compound leaves. This means there is more than one leaf attached to each leaf stem. Their flowers usually have petals that are separated from one another. The flowers of roses and their relatives also tend to develop in the same ways. Roses, hawthorns, apples, peaches, cherries, pears, plums, strawberries, and raspberries are all in this group.

Red, red roses

One of the most popular flowers today is the red rose. Would you believe that until 1930, there were no red roses? Most roses that you see are **cultivated** roses. These are roses that people have developed to produce specific kinds of flowers. In 1930, the first red rose appeared. The color of a plant's flowers is determined by the plant's **genes.** Roses do not usually have a gene for red flower color. But in 1930, something happened by chance to the genes of a rose plant, and it grew red flowers. Since then, rose growers have used that rose plant's **descendants** to make new rose plants with red roses.

These are all cultivated roses. They come in red, white, yellow, pink, orange, and lavender. No wild rose plants make red or blue flowers. Scientists are working on making a cultivated rose plant with blue roses.

Monster flowers

Imagine a flower almost as wide as you are tall. The giant rafflesia makes the largest known flowers. Its flowers can have a diameter as wide as 3 feet, 3 inches (1 meter)—that's about as wide as a 3-year-old child is tall. These huge flowers smell like rotting meat. This smell attracts the flies that pollinate the flowers. This stinky plant is **classified** in its own order.

Parasitic plants

Giant rafflesias and other plants in their order are **parasites.** Unlike most other plants, they do not carry out **photosynthesis.** Instead, they get **nutrients** by living off other plants.

Unless you see one of the flowers of these parasites, you might never notice the plant at all. These plants are not green, and they do not have typical roots, stems, or leaves. Except for their flowers, these plants tend to live completely inside the stems and roots of other plants. If you were to cut open the **host** plant, the plant parasite living inside might look similar to a tangle of threads.

*The huge flowers of the giant rafflesia plant stay open for about one week. During this time, flies **pollinate** it.*

Peas in a Pod

About 18,000 **species** of plants are legumes. Their flowers contain only one **pistil**. Their **fruits** are called pods. When ripe, the pod splits open and releases the **seeds.** Legumes make up another **order** of **dicots.**

Making food for you and me

If you have ever eaten peanut butter, then you have eaten the product of a legume. Legumes are important in the world for the production of food for humans and for animals that are raised to feed humans. Foods made from legumes are high in protein and fat. These **nutrients** are necessary for human growth. Peanuts, chick peas, lentils, soybeans, and other beans and peas are all foods from legume fruits. Alfalfa and clover are legumes used to feed animals.

Peas are the fruit of pea plants. About 5 to 10 peas grow inside a pod like the one shown here.

Nitrogen-fixing bacteria live in these ball-shaped structures on the roots of legume plants. The plants give the bacteria a home and food. In return, the bacteria provide the plant and other living things with nitrogen.

Fixing nitrogen

Have you ever heard of someone **fertilizing** a plant? When you fertilize a plant, you give it nutrients, most importantly **nitrogen,** in a form it can use to grow. Legumes have their own fertilizer factories in their roots!

Legumes have swollen bumps on their roots where the **bacteria** live. These bacteria take nitrogen and change it into a form that plants can use to live and grow. Animals and other living things then get that nitrogen by eating plants.

Helpful legumes

All living things need nitrogen to live. Nitrogen is used to make hair, skin, and fingernails. It is also an important part of **genetic** material. But most of the nitrogen in the world is in a form that living things cannot use. Nitrogen-fixing bacteria unlock this nitrogen. Without nitrogen-fixing bacteria, living things would run out of nitrogen. In this way, legume plants help all other plants and animals around them get nitrogen.

Palms and Their Relatives

You have probably seen palms in the movies, or maybe in person. Palms grow in warm, wet places, such as along beaches and in tropical areas. Their leaves are usually fan-shaped or feather-shaped. If you look closely at the leaves, you will notice that they have parallel **veins.** This and other characteristics of palms tell you that these plants are **monocots.** They make up an ancient **order** of plants that have lived on Earth for more than 110 million years.

Unlike the roots of trees, palm roots do not get thicker as they grow. Often, you can find a cone of roots at the base of a palm tree.

Not real trees

You may have heard palms called "palm trees." Palms grow tall like trees, but they are not like other trees. A palm usually has a tall trunk that is about the same diameter from ground to "tree" top. In fact, the trunk often reaches its full width before the plant grows above ground. The trunks of most trees get wider each year, but the trunks of palms do not. Also unlike most trees, palms rarely have branches.

Palm flowers and fruits

Members of this group usually have small flowers. Many tiny flowers grow off one branch. Some palms grow only male or female flowers. Others have both male and female flowers. Palms are **pollinated** in many different ways.

In some palms, wind carries the **pollen**. Bees, flies, beetles, and even bats pollinate other palms. Palm **fruits** are usually berries with one **seed** or a fleshy fruit with one pit, or stone, inside. A coconut is an example of a fleshy palm fruit.

All-purpose plant

For hundreds of years, people living near palms have used them in many different ways. For example, palm trunks are used to construct buildings and furniture. Their leaves and husks are used to make ropes, mats, and thatched roofs. Parts of their fruits are used to make charcoal, cups, and bottles. Other fruits, such as dates, hearts of palm, and coconuts, are eaten as food. Their oils and juices are used in cooking. Palms are also used for decoration, especially in resorts along beaches.

Counting leaves

Some palms are very old. It is not unusual for a palm to live to be 50 or 100 years old. Palms in the Seychelles, a group of islands near eastern Africa, are thought to be 350 years old. In Australia, palms have lived as long as 720 years. The age of a palm can be estimated. If you know how long it takes a palm to grow one leaf, you can count the scars on the stem left from past leaves that have fallen off.

All of a palm's leaves grow at the top. Only a set number of leaves can grow on a palm. A new leaf does not begin to grow until an existing one dies.

Grasses, Sedges, and Their Relatives

Grasses, sedges, cattails, and other similar plants are also **monocots.** They all tend to have long, flat leaves and tall stems. These plants make small flowers without **nectar.** Their flowers are **pollinated** by wind.

Grasses

You are probably more familiar with grasses than you think. You see grasses growing on lawns and in parks. But did you know that you eat grass **fruits** every day? Rice, wheat, barley, rye, oats, and corn all come from grass plants. Cereal plants like these are the most important source of food in the world. About half of the energy that people get from food comes from grass plants.

Grasses spread easily and are hard to get rid of. Grasses can grow in areas too dry for trees and form grasslands, such as a prairie. Grasses can also **reproduce** through underground stems, called **rhizomes.** If the top off a grass plant is cut off by a lawn mower or by a grazing animal, it does not die. The part of the grass plant that grows is very low on the plant and is not disturbed by cutting the tips off.

*Wheat flowers do not have petals or **sepals.** The grain is ground into flour, which is then used to make bread.*

Sedges

Most sedges grow in wet places, such as on the shores of ponds and lakes and in marshes and swamps. Some sedges have stems and leaves that are hard to tear. They are used around the world to weave mats, baskets, and even to make sandals. Ancient Egyptians, Greeks, and Romans used a sedge plant, called papyrus, to make writing paper and books.

Sedges are the main plants in many wetlands around the world. Their fruits and other plant parts provide food for wetland animals. Their stems and leaves provide homes and hiding places for these animals.

Cattails

You have probably seen cattails growing beside a pond. Cattails have tall stems and long, flat leaves. Their leaves can be weaved into mats, baskets, and the seats of chairs. Cattail flowers have no petals at all. The brown part of a cattail contains the female flowers. The thinner, yellow part contains the male flowers. Wind or water carries cattail **seeds** to new places. All parts of cattails can be eaten. The yellow **pollen** of cattails can be added to cookie dough or pancake batter to make them taste better. Cattail stems can be used in salads. Their young green flower spikes can be cooked and eaten just like corn on the cob.

You can tell sedges from grasses by cutting the stem across. When cut, a sedge stem end looks like a solid triangle. Grass stems usually look like hollow circles when cut in half.

Worst weed in the world

Weeds are any unwanted plant. You have probably seen weeds growing in a garden. Many sedges are weeds. Because sedges are good at growing in new places and can quickly spread out, they are common weeds. For example, purple nut sedge grows among crops in warm areas of the world. It is sometimes called the worst weed in the world because of all the damage it can cause.

Bromeliads and Bananas

Bromeliads, pineapples, bananas, ginger, and prayer plants are another group of **monocots.** Most bromeliads have short stems and pointed leaves with spines along the edges. The leaves overlap like the petals on a rose. Almost all bromeliads are native to North and South America and the West Indies.

Air plants

About half of all bromeliads are **epiphytes,** or air plants. Epiphytes are plants whose roots grow on other plants or in the air. They commonly grow in humid **climates.** Epiphytes are not **parasites.** They collect water from the plants they grow on in cuplike tanks formed by their leaves. The largest tank bromeliads hold as much as 5 gallons (20 liters) of water—enough liquid to fill five one-gallon milk jugs.

Rainforest aquarium

The water-holding tanks formed by some bromeliad leaves can be compared to an aquarium. Hundreds of different kinds of organisms have been found living in bromeliad tanks, including **protozoa,** insects, spiders, scorpions, mites, worms, frogs, salamanders, snakes, and the mosquito that causes **malaria.**

The parts of a bromeliad

The roots of bromeliads that grow on rocks or on other plants hold the plant in place. These roots usually do not take in water or

Bromeliads often have flowers at the end of a long spike. The leaves along the spike are also brightly colored.

nutrients for the plant. Some bromeliads have no roots at all. The leaves of most epiphytic bromeliads do the job that roots normally do. They can take in water and nutrients. Bromeliads are **pollinated** mostly by hummingbirds. These birds are attracted to the flowers' **nectar.**

Bananas

Banana plants look like small trees, but they are not real trees. The part that looks like a trunk is made thick by layers of many large leaves. A large spike with many yellow flowers grows at the top of the plant and bends down toward the ground. One spike of flowers can grow into a bunch of 50 to 150 bananas. Each banana plant can produce only one bunch of bananas. Once a banana plant grows a bunch of bananas, the plant is usually cut down.

Bananas are one of the most important food crops in the world. Bananas are usually grown in warm areas, such as in Central and South America, and then shipped to markets in North America and around the world. Bananas are picked while they are still green so that they will become ripe after they arrive at the market.

This frog has found a home in a water tank bromeliad.

Lilies, Orchids, and Their Relatives

Lilies, orchids, and their relatives form the largest group of **monocots.** Many of these plants have large, brightly colored flowers and sweet-smelling **nectar.** The flowers usually do not have green **sepals** under the flower petals. Instead, the sepals may resemble the petals. Animals usually **pollinate** these flowers. Leaves of these plants are long and thin and have parallel **veins.**

Members of this group include many familiar garden plants, such as irises, gladiolus, crocuses, narcissus, amaryllis, tulips, aloe plants, lilies, and orchids. Onion, garlic, leeks, shallots, and asparagus are plants in this group that are commonly eaten. Vanilla and saffron spices also come from plants in this group.

Underground parts

The underground parts of these plants mainly store food and water. **Rhizomes** and **corms** are underground stems. New plants can grow from these structures. For example, irises grow from rhizomes. Crocuses and gladiolus grow from corms.

Bulbs are round, underground buds surrounded by leaves. Onions are a good example of a bulb. The outside

This narcissus bulb is sprouting. The round part of the bulb at the bottom is made up of leaves that store food for the plant. The stems coming out of the top are the new growth.

part of an onion is thin like paper. This papery covering protects the leaves inside. A bulb's leaves contain food that allows a plant to wait to grow until water is available. For example, during winter or when there is little rain, a bulb can feed itself until water becomes available.

Pollinators

Animals—mostly bees and other insects—commonly pollinate the flowers of orchids, lilies, and their relatives. Bees are attracted to the bright colors and sweet smells of the flowers. Some flowers even have nectar guides which are special markings on flowers that direct bees to the **pollen** inside the flower. Birds sometimes pollinate a few plants in this group that have a distinctive flower pattern and color.

Orchids

The best place to find an orchid growing naturally is in a cloud forest. Cloud forests are wet and misty most of the time. This is the perfect climate for orchids, especially those growing on other plants. Orchid **epiphytes** take in water from the air.

This orchid looks similar to a female wasp. Male wasps pollinate the flowers when trying to mate with them.

Recognizing Flowering Plants

Even though flowering plants come in many shapes and sizes and have very different ways of life, they are all **classified** as **angiosperms**. Angiosperms have one main thing in common: they all make flowers and **fruits.** These plants are all classified in their own **division** within the plant **kingdom.**

In some angiosperms, the leaves are more colorful and showy than the flowers are. The leaves of caladiums, for example, are bright and colorful, while the flowers are plain. Many gardeners remove the flowers as soon as they appear, so that the plant will not spend energy growing them. Then, the plant will spend its energy making the prettier leaves.

Recognizing flowers

Using the test of whether a plant makes flowers or not helps to recognize flowering plants. However, it is not always that easy, because there are so many different kinds of flowers. As you have seen in this book, flowers come in all sizes, forms, and colors.

The flowers of magnolias, gladiolus, poppies, tulips, daylilies, irises, and many other flowers have large, colorful petals. They look like typical flowers. Other common flowers, such as sunflowers, asters, and chrysanthemums, are actually small flowers growing close together. But they still look like pretty flowers. Other plants, however, have flowers that are not showy at all. For example, cauliflower and broccoli are tight clusters of flower buds. Grasses, sedges, wheat, rice, and rye are other examples of plants with tiny, plain flowers.

It is not the color or the size of the flower that matters. All plants that make flowers are angiosperms and are classified in this division. All other plants are non-flowering plants and are classified in different plant divisions.

Looking for fruits and seeds

Flowers are the **reproductive** parts of flowering plants. When a plant reproduces with its flowers, it makes **seeds,** which are enclosed in a fruit. Since the plant uses flowers mainly for reproduction, most flowers last just a short time. That means that you might come across a flowering plant during a time when it is not in bloom. How might you tell if a plant is an angiosperm if it is not in bloom?

One way to recognize angiosperms is to look for their fruits. Plants with fruits, such as bananas, apples, and oranges, are angiosperms. Of course, not all fruits look the same. Some do not look like the fruits you are likely to put in a fruit salad. Grains are fruits, for example. So are acorns and nuts.

Fruits develop from flowers. The flowers on this zucchini plant are wilting as the zucchinis grow out of them. The plant's seeds are inside of zucchinis. If you have ever eaten a zucchini, then you have seen the seeds.

Only angiosperms enclose their seeds in fruits. The other seed plants—**gymnosperms**—have naked seeds. So if a plant makes fruits with seeds inside, it is an angiosperm.

What about the plants that make seedless grapes and seedless watermelons? Scientists have bred these plants to make fruits without seeds. Normally, these plants would make seeds in their fruits. Some still do, but the seeds are so small that we do not notice them when we eat the fruits. The **ancestors** and wild relatives of these plants still make seeds in their fruits. The **classification** system is clear and consistent. Plants that make flowers and fruits are angiosperms. Those that do not are classified in different divisions.

Glossary

adaptation special feature that helps a plant survive in its habitat

ancestor plant relative that lived long ago

angiosperm flowering plant

bacteria single-celled organism that does not have a nucleus

bulb underground resting form of a plant which consists of a short stem with one or more buds surrounded by thick leaves

burr rough or prickly covering or shell of a seed or fruit

cell smallest unit of life

class level of classification that contains similar orders

classify group organisms into categories based on their similar characteristics

climate weather conditions that are usual for a certain area

complete flower flower that has sepals, petals, stamens, and pistils

corm short, swollen underground plant stem

cotyledon seed leaves a plant grows when it is still an embryo inside the seed

cultivated not wild or natural

deciduous loses leaves each year

descendant later generation of a type of organism

dicot plant with two seed leaves

digest process by which a plant breaks down food so it can be absorbed

digestive system group of organs that break down food so it can be used by the body

division level of classification that contains similar classes

embryo structure formed when an egg and a sperm join together

epiphyte any plant that grows on another plant or an object above ground and has no roots in soil

extinct no longer on Earth

family level of classification that contains similar genera

fertilizing adding material to the soil to make it better able to produce

fossil remains of ancient living organism found in rocks

fruit enlarged female reproductive part of a flowering plant. It contains and protects the seeds of flowering plants.

fungi any of a large group of plantlike organisms that must live on other plants or animals or decaying material

gene structure by which all living things pass on characteristics to the next generation

genus (plural is **genera**) level of classification that contains similar species

gymnosperm earliest seed plants

habitat place where an organism lives

host plant on which a parasite lives and feeds from

imperfect flower flower that has only female or male reproductive parts

incomplete flower missing either sepals, petals, stamens, or pistils

kingdom level of classification that contains similar phyla or divisions

malaria serious disease spread by the bite of a mosquito

mineral solid substance formed in the earth by nature

monocot plant with one seed leaf

nectar sweet liquid produced by some flowers

nitrogen colorless, odorless gaseous chemical element that makes up 78 percent of the atmosphere and forms a part of all living tissue

nutrient chemical that helps plants grow and carry out life processes

order level of classification that contains similar families

parasite living thing that lives and feeds on or inside another living thing

perfect flower flower that has both male and female reproductive parts

photosynthesis process by which plants use carbon dioxide in the air and energy from sunlight to make food in the form of sugars

phylum (plural is **phyla**) level of classification that contains similar classes

pistil female reproductive part of a flower

pollen dustlike particles that contain sperm

pollination transfer of pollen from male to female flower parts

predator animal that hunts and eats other animals

prey animal that is hunted and eaten by other animals

protozoa one of a large group of microscopic beings made up of a single cell

reproduce produce another living thing of the same kind

rhizome underground stem that looks like a root and holds the plant in the soil

seed structure that contains an undeveloped plant and stored food that the plant needs to grow

sepal part of a flower that surrounds and protects the flower before it blooms

species level of classification that contains similar organisms

stamen male reproductive part of a flower

tuber short, fleshy underground stem

vein bundles of tubes in a leaf that transports water and nutrients

whorl sepals, petals, stamens, and/or pistils

More Books to Read

Greenaway, Theresa. *The Plant Kingdom*. Austin, Tex.: Raintree Steck-Vaughn, 1999.

Hewitt, Sally, et al. *Plants*. Brookfield, Conn.: Millbrook Press, Inc., 2001.

Snedden, Robert. *Plants and Fungi*. Chicago: Heinemann Library, 2002.

Index